structu

nature

FlipDesigns®

graffiti

elements

colors

Front jacket: Sailboat off Santa Cruz, California USA

Back jacket: Drainpipe, Italy

Prestel-Verlag
Mandlstrasse 26, D-80802 Munich, Germany
Tel.: (89) 38-17-09-0, Fax.: (89) 38-17-09-35
www.prestel.de

4 Bloomsbury Place, London, WC1A 2QA
Tel.: (020) 7323 5004, Fax.: (020) 7636 8004

175 Fifth Avenue, Suite 402, New York, NY 10010
Tel.: (212) 995 2720, Fax.: (212) 995 2733
www.prestel.com

Library of Congress Card Number: 00-111851

Prestel books are available worldwide. Please contact your
nearest bookseller or any of the above addresses for information
concerning your local distributor.

Editorial direction: Philippa Hurd

Design and typesetting: WIGEL, Munich
Printed and bound by peradruck, Gräfelfing

Printed in Germany
ISBN: 3-7913-2481-0

FlipDesigns®

MICHAEL JENNER

Prestel
Munich · London · New York

Introduction

It all began when I was repairing the Spanish Steps. I had been cataloguing and digitizing my photographic archive when I came across some pictures of the magnificent staircase leading up to the church of Trinità dei Monti in Rome. I remember having spent a night or two in the 1970s wandering the streets of the Eternal City laden with cameras and tripod in search of these and other motifs. For some reason, I had shot only one frame each of three different views of the Spanish Steps. They had all turned out pretty well, except that the best one was scarred by an ugly gash due to a careless mishap in a Roman darkroom. In short, the picture was ruined. Unusable, the negative had lain untouched for almost a quarter of a century until today's technical wonders made it possible with a series of copy-and-paste commands to repair the damage.

Then I began to do other things to the Spanish Steps, flipping the image this way and that. A double staircase emerged that was a delight to behold. I added another. Soon I had steps going in all directions and doubling back on themselves. My eyes scampered eagerly up and down these enticing perspectives. As I repeated and refined the process, gradually the original object of stone steps by moonlight came adrift from its context and dissolved into a mysterious pattern. A different type of image had come into being. I knew I was on to something.

So I abandoned my archiving of travel photography. Instead, I searched for specific images, the ones with the magic to create compelling patterns. There was no shortage of material. For even while taking pictures for books and magazines of the conventional descriptive kind, I had been drawn time and again to abstract shapes, bold colors, and geometric structures. This kind of photography had always attracted me, albeit as an essentially private indulgence. Now, as I trawled through my archive, everything started to make sense. As if their hour had come at last, long-forgotten pictures floated back to the surface, caught my eye, and lined up for attention alongside more recent efforts. I realized I had been searching for patterns all along. But I had only been able to record the starting point. Digital technology would now allow me to pick up the individual building blocks and to take things forward to their proper conclusion. I worked with a frenzy: sorting, scanning and shaping images. I was bombarded with ideas from many

Spanish Steps by Moonlight, Rome, Italy

varied sources: the curved colonnade of St. Peter's in Rome, the dome of St. Basil's in Moscow, the stone gardens of Japanese temples in Kyoto, a shuttered beach hut in Rimini, dyed textiles from the Sahara, the veins of a fallen leaf in North America, a post-modern façade in Berlin, a row of colored deckchairs in Oxford.

At first, I felt a pattern could be made out of almost anything. Fresh visions seemed to jump out with every twist of the kaleidoscope. But it soon became clear that to reach a successful result the basic image had to be carefully chosen, tweaked, and cropped over and over until it was just right. For the smallest disruptive element could set off minor patterns of its own that rarely agreed with the logic of the whole. Often I abandoned what had seemed so promising because the design was going nowhere. But generally, I persisted and wrestled my way into the very heart of the pattern, agonizing over tiny details, until the last pixel was nudged into position and the whole thing suddenly locked into place like matching samples of DNA. This was the most rewarding part of it all, seeing things finally come together in a truly satisfying composition.

Strange things happened in the process. As patterns evolved, outlines of butterflies emerged from leaves, hazy faces peered out from rust stains, elegant birds took flight from crude daubs of paint on a wall, luscious crimson lips were born from a menacing hammer and sickle. Materials transmuted. Stone became parchment. Sand assumed the texture of canvas. Spring flowers in a meadow turned into bright stitches on a medieval tapestry. A bed of red tulips ignited like a bushfire. Even smudges of dirt could serve as artistic shading. Although an optical experience, it was one that fully engaged the senses. After a session immersed in red hot lava from the crater of Mount Etna, I plunged with relief into the cool blue of swimming pools, chilled out in the soothing azure of the sky, or in the leafy green of the forest.

Knowing when to stop was another matter. With the full arsenal of computer graphics at my disposal, the possibilities were endless. I could flatten mountains and stand them on their head, fashion a necklace out of moonbeams, make the ocean flow against the tide. I could travel back in time, replant Catherine the Great's garden at Tsarskoe Selo or redesign a window of Stockholm City Hall. I could flout all rules of structural engineering and launch digitally modified copies of Milan cathedral through the heavens like a surreal squadron of Gothic spaceships: real architectural lift-off at last.

At times I imagined not just framed pictures on a wall but entire rooms covered with a kind of fantasy wallpaper that was so powerful it would be worth framing in its own right. But, in contrast to traditional wallpaper designs that build up various bits of detail into a bigger figurative image, almost the opposite was happening here. For what began as a natural element—for example a flower petal—soon became decidedly deconstructed and transmuted into something else. So although the final product might be informed by nature and speak the language of nature, the artifice of replication made it anything but natural in the usual sense of the word. Thus a curious ambivalence arose between point of origin and end result, superimposing a disorientating layer of uncertainty.

Other thoughts and questions occurred too. Why from the earliest times has the human eye displayed such hunger for patterns, as evidenced in the triple spiral at prehistoric Newgrange in Ireland, the repetitive decoration of the Ishtar Gate in Babylon, or the interlacing fretwork on classical Greek temples? Perhaps, in order to perceive one thing properly, we need to see it many times over before it can take definitive shape in the mind's eye? Or do we tune in instinctively to patterns and go in search of symmetrical repetition as part of an endless quest to find divine order and absolute perfection in a chaotic universe? For in a pattern the seemingly impossible becomes possible. Without any contradiction, things can go apart and come together in a continuum where opposites forever meet, merge, and move on. And ultimately all discordance is reconciled.

The act of making these images has certainly changed the way I see physical reality. I now note the basic stuff of patterns all around. I find myself consciously taking photo-graphs that will permit the creation of new patterns. I look beyond the self-evident aspect of the single object that faces the camera lens and try to guess what sort of pattern will evolve. Sometimes I buy fruit and vegetables just for their visual qualities. The cross-section of a red onion or a ripe tomato can set my pulse racing. Sometimes, when con-fronted with an unlikely subject such as a broken pavement or an ordinary domestic drainpipe, I feel a real thrill like that of a medieval alchemist suddenly possessed with the crazy notion of turning base metal into gold.

But how to classify these FlipDesigns®? For me they are a novel and exciting encounter between abstract photography, digital technology, and graphic design. In one sense what is happening here is still essentially photography, but not as I have known it previ-ously. Yet in a certain sense, these images are actually closer to the literal sense of the Greek words meaning "writing with light" than is the straightforward photographic act, which simply records with light. Perhaps this area could be known as photo-graphics, with the deliberate addition of the hyphen in order to give each part of the word its full value. Anyway, one thing is clear: the interaction of camera and computer opens up many new possibilities of expression and perception that will continue to blur and erode the old borderlines between photography and design.

01 / Four Deckchairs, Oxford, England

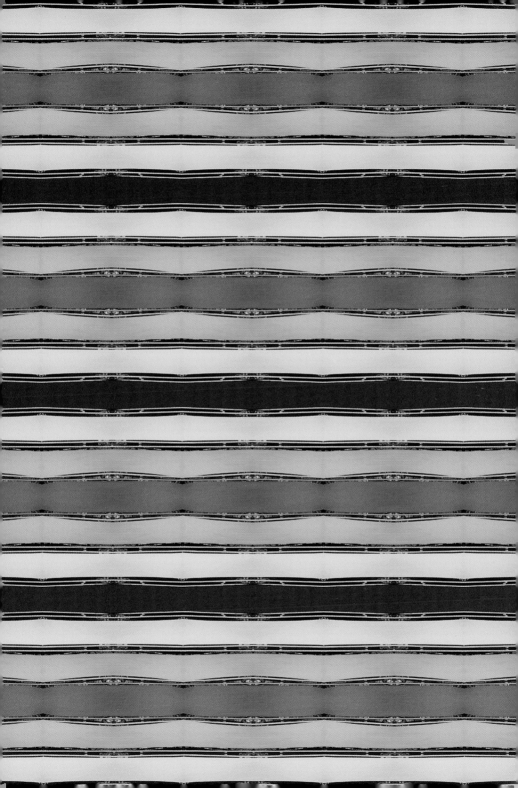

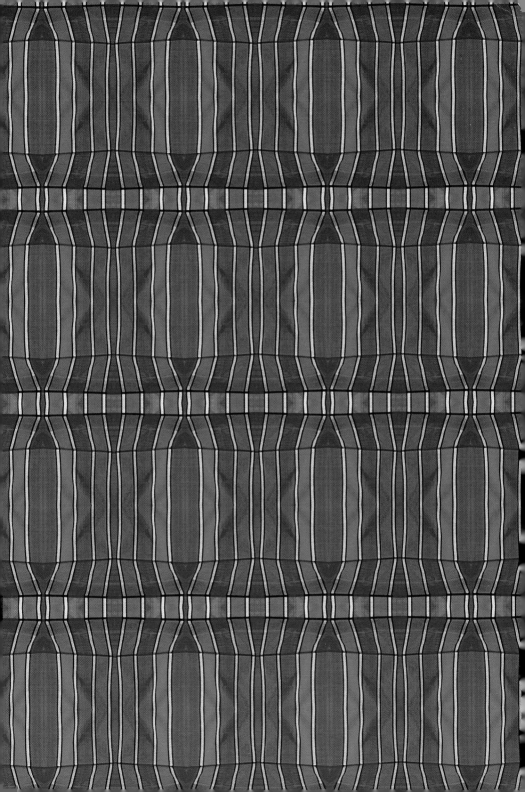

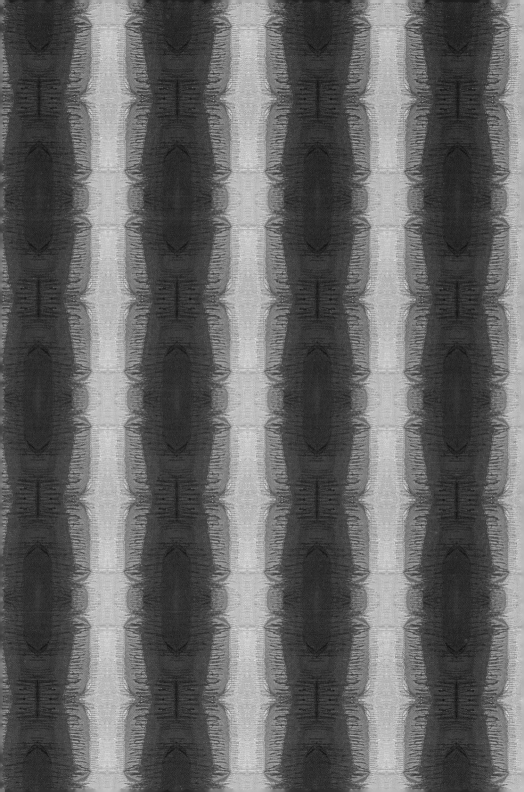

04 / Saharan Textiles, Tunisia

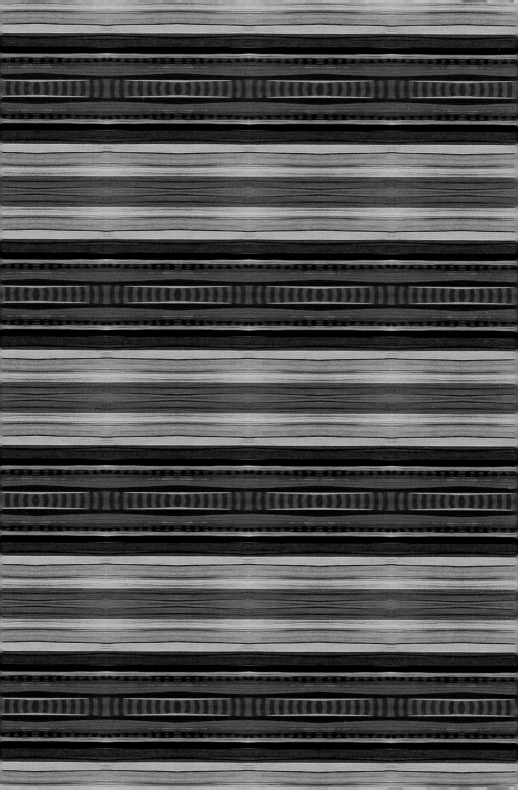

05 / Wall and Door Frame, Italy

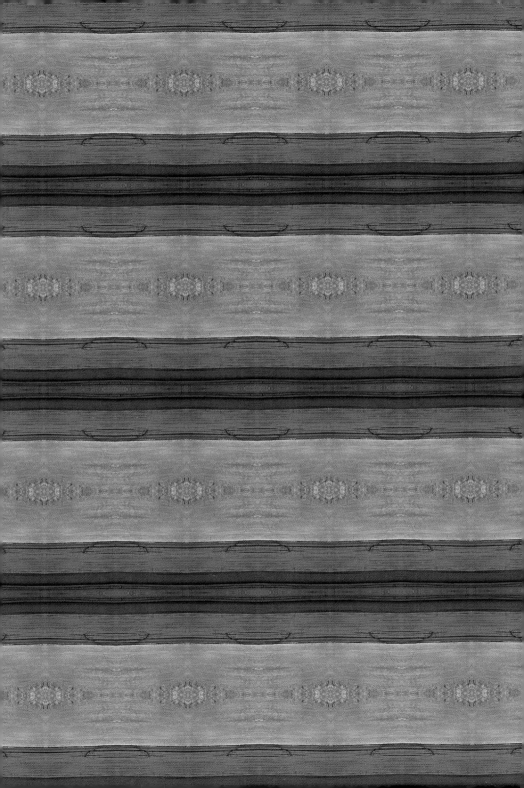

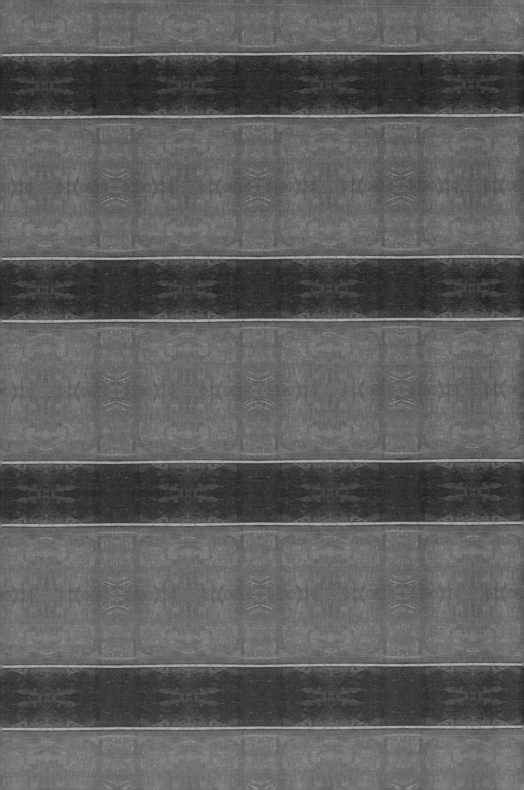

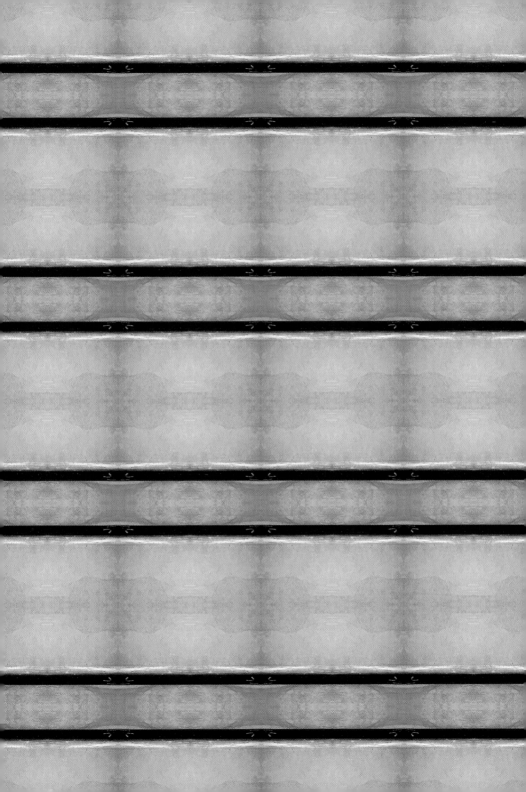

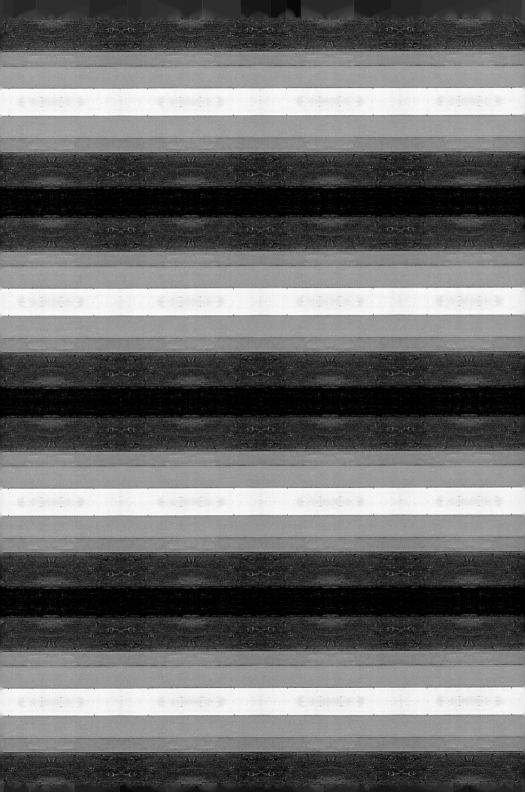

11 / Windbreak, Lee-on-the-Solent, England

15 / Spray-paint on Metal, Rome, Italy

17 / Graffiti (1), Rome, Italy

18 / Graffiti (2), Rome, Italy

ER NON FAR
I ARGAN
LCUNI MESI F
ER ESSERSI R(

19 / Graffiti (3), Rome, Italy

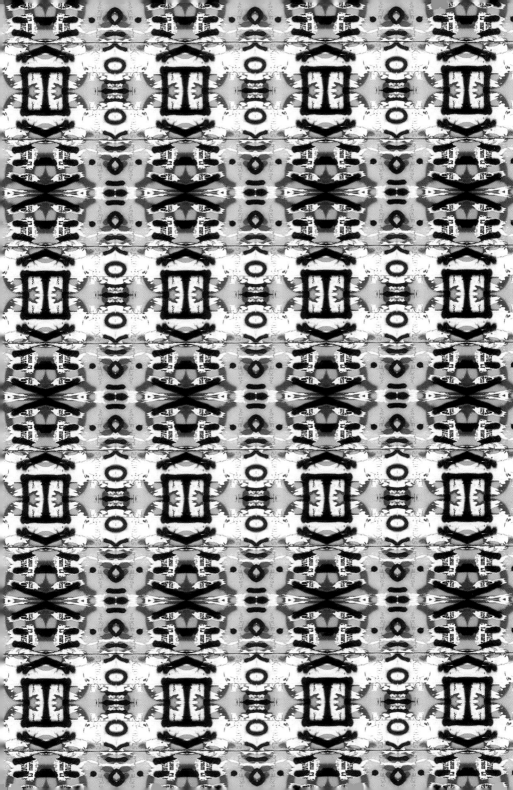

21 / Graffiti (5), Rome, Italy

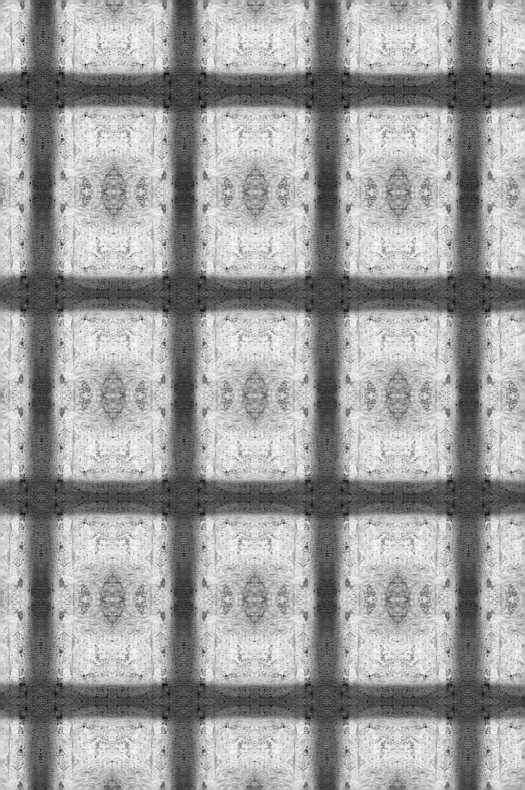

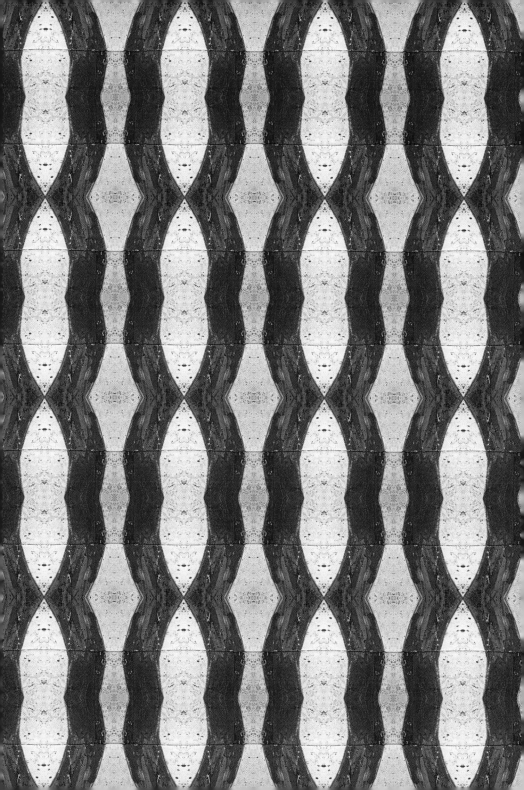

23 / Graffiti (7), Rome, Italy

24 / Red Onion (1)

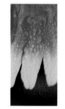

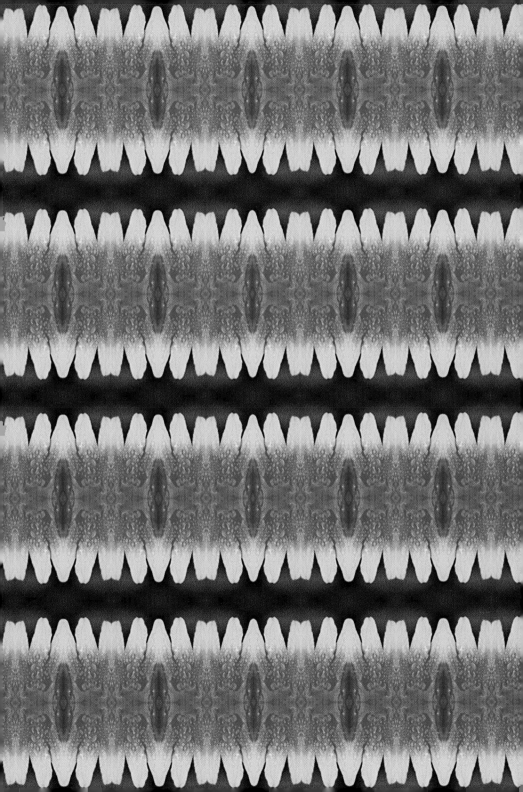

34 / Croton Leaves, Seychelles

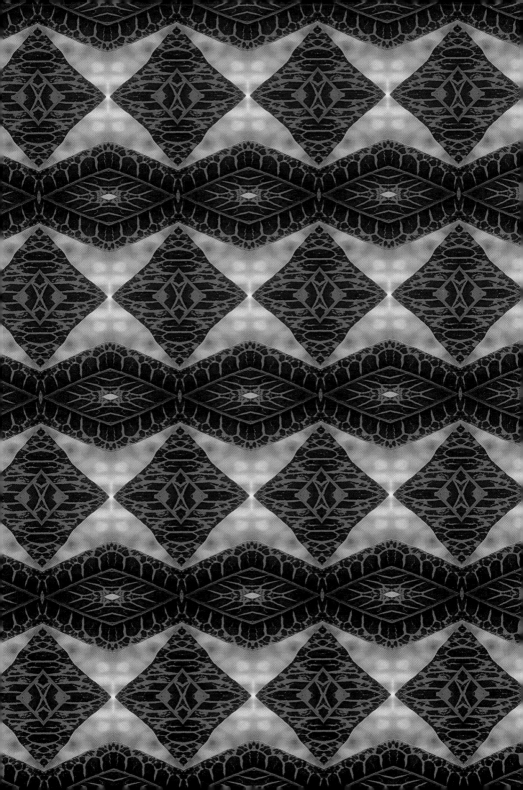

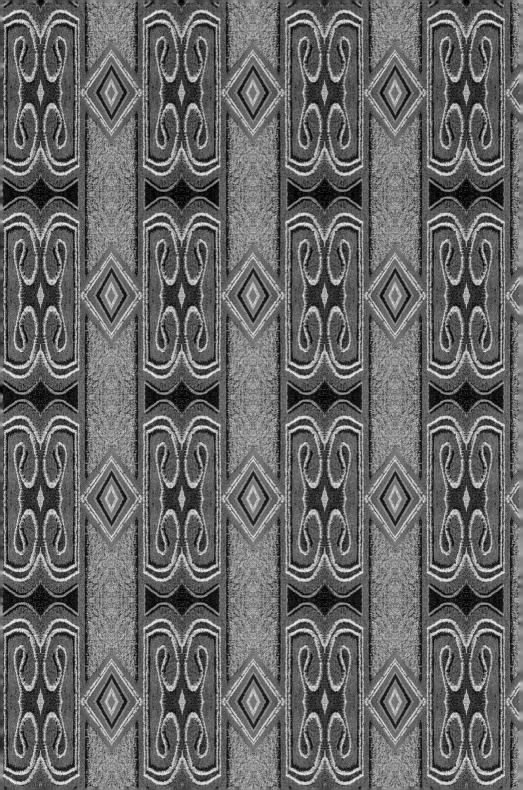

41 / Peacock, Kew Gardens, London, England

47 / Paper Lantern in Cherry Tree, Miyajima, Japan

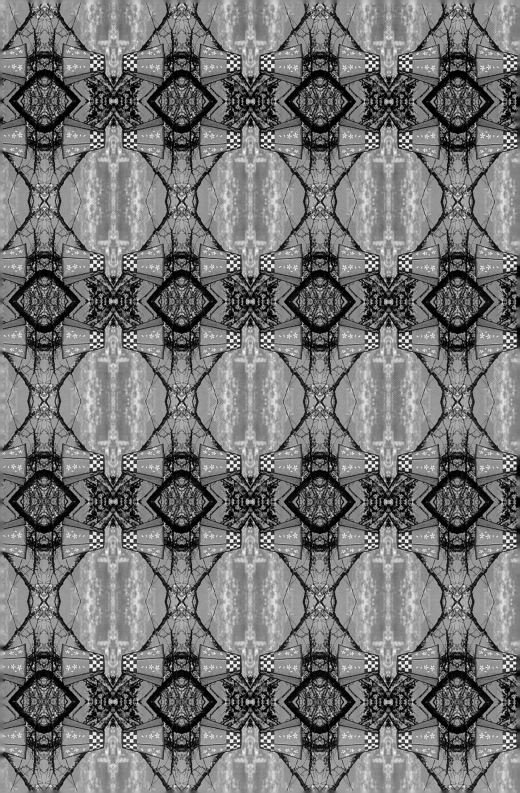

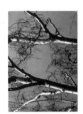

49 / Yosemite National Park, California, USA

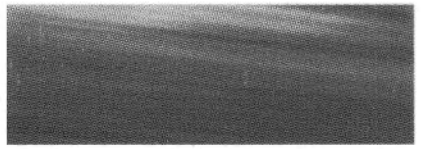

53 / Lava Flow (1), Mount Etna, Sicily

57 / Aegean Moon, Greece

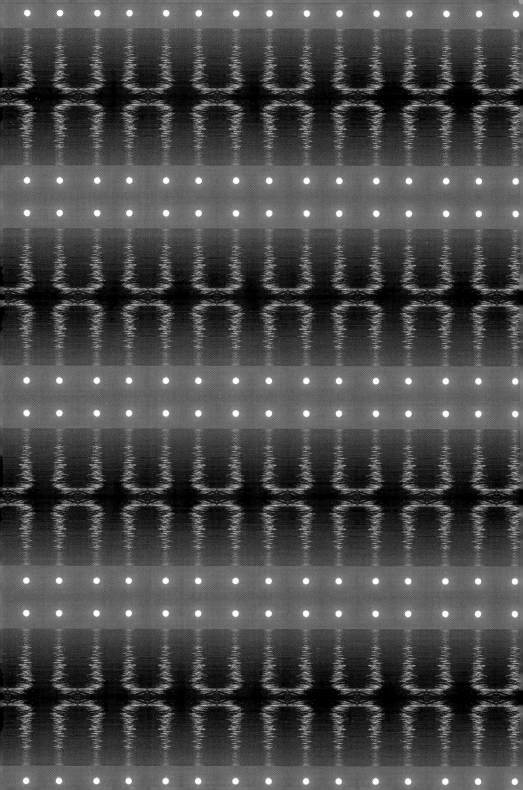

61 / Pool, Manama, Bahrain

65 / Blue Wall with Pipes, Bahrain

68 / Colored Ribbons, Peace Park, Hiroshima, Japan

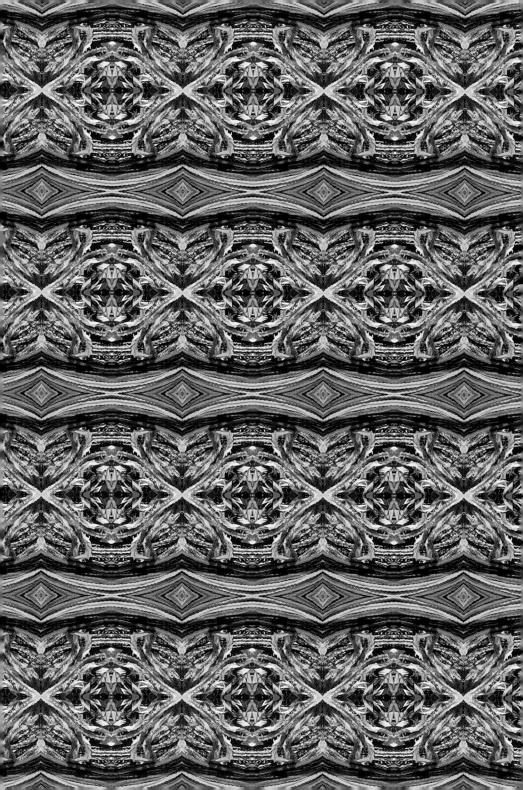

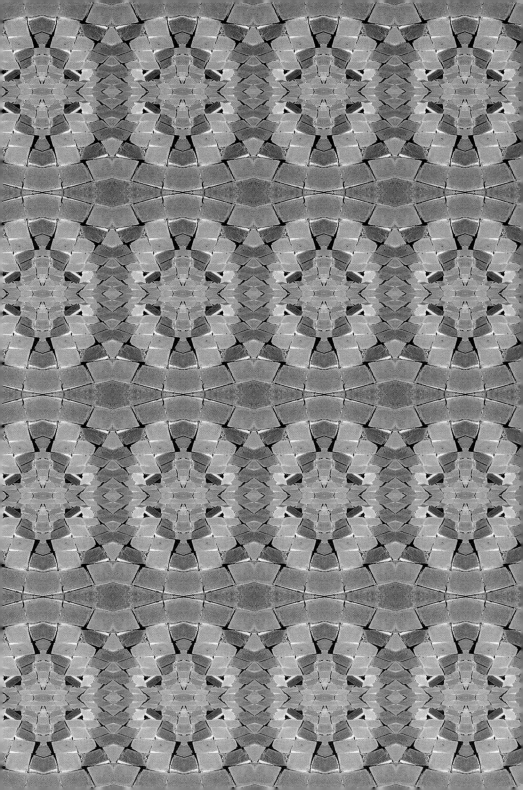

71 / Dam on Euphrates, Al-Thawra, Syria

72 / Castle Stair, Krak des Chevaliers, Syria

74 / Oriental Brickwork, Tozeur, Tunisia

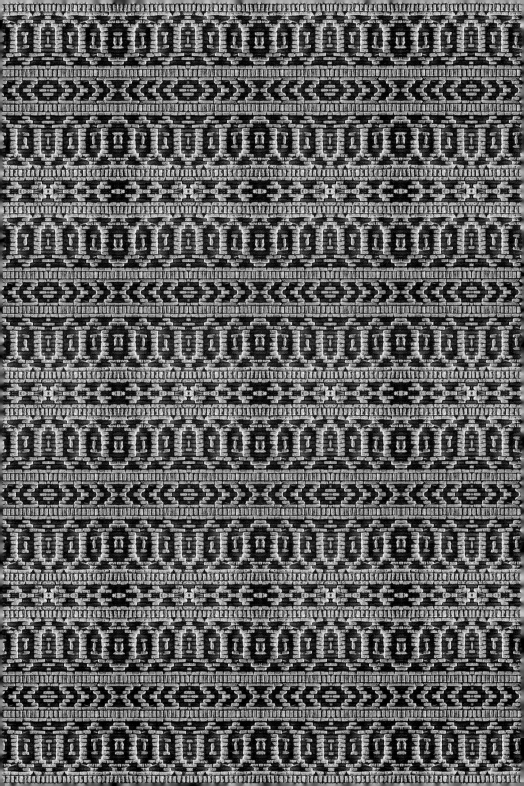

76 / Window, Stockholm City Hall, Sweden

80 / Window, London, England

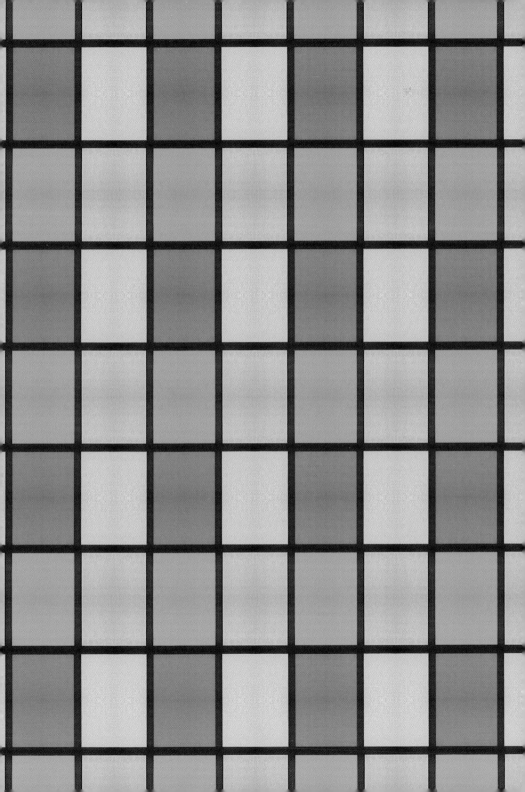

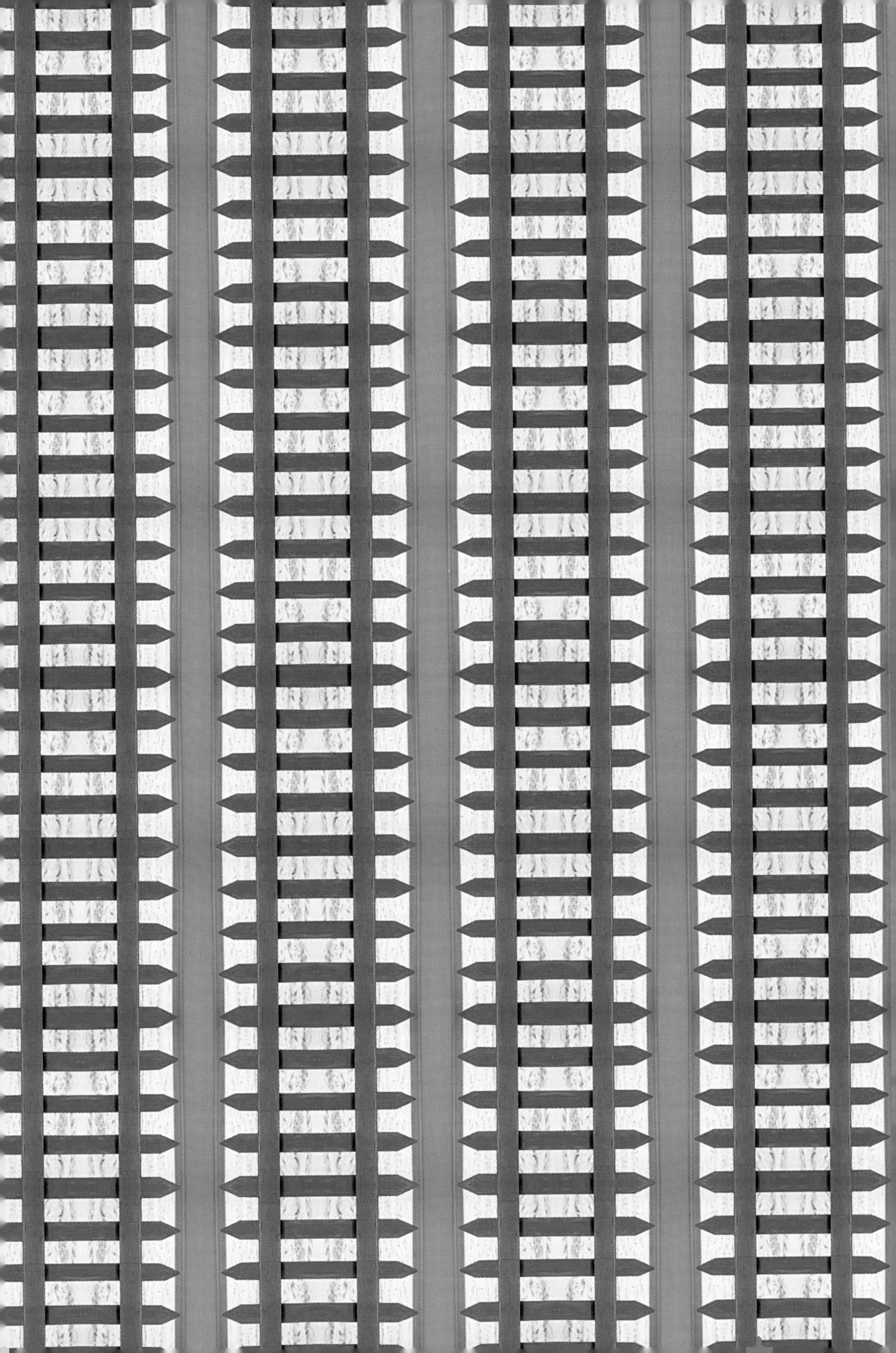

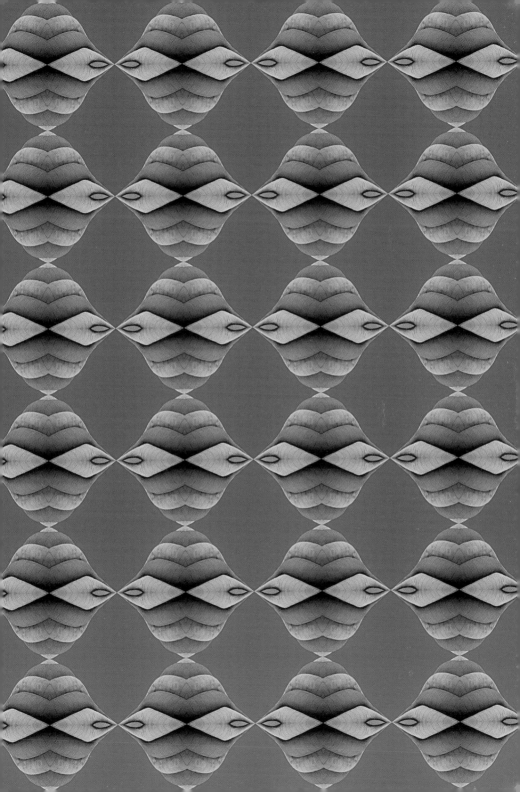

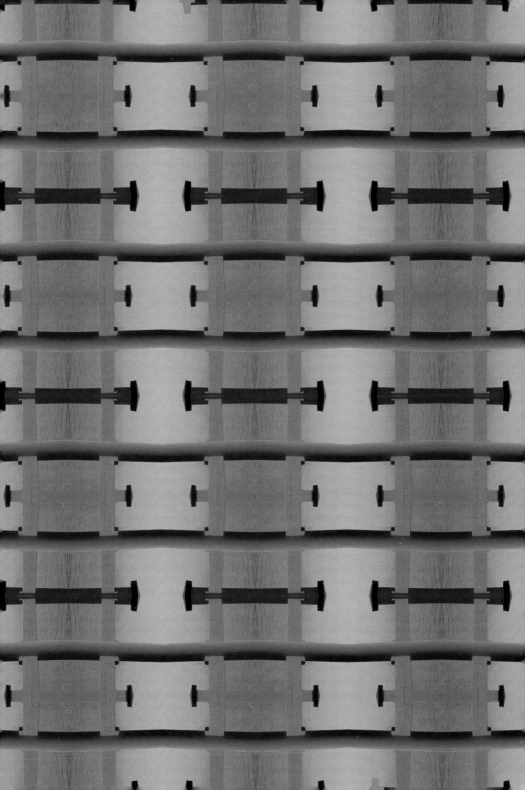

01 / Four Deckchairs, Oxford, England
02 / Windbreak, Cornwall, England
03 / Textile Souk, Marrakesh, Morocco
04 / Saharan Textiles, Tunisia
05 / Wall and Door Frame, Italy
06 / Beach Hut (1), Adriatic Coast, Italy
07 / Pink Wall Black Drainpipe, Italy
08 / Beach Hut (2), Adriatic Coast, Italy
09 / Beach Hut (3), Adriatic Coast, Italy
10 / Beach Hut (4), Adriatic Coast, Italy
11 / Windbreak, Lee-on-the-Solent, England
12 / Building-site Billboard, Italy
13 / Poster on Wall, Rome, Italy
14 / Spray-paint on Newspaper, Rome, Italy
15 / Spray-paint on Metal, Rome, Italy
16 / Spray-paint on Wood, Rome, Italy
17 / Graffiti (1), Rome, Italy
18 / Graffiti (2), Rome, Italy
19 / Graffiti (3), Rome, Italy
20 / Graffiti (4), Rome, Italy
21 / Graffiti (5), Rome, Italy
22 / Graffiti (6), Rome, Italy
23 / Graffiti (7), Rome, Italy
24 / Red Onion (1)
25 / Red Onion (2)
26 / Red Onion (3)
27 / Tomato
28 / Red Leaf
29 / Hydrangea Leaf
30 / Tropical Leaf, Seychelles
31 / Heliconia, Seychelles

32 / Canna Lily, Liguria, Italy
33 / Gaillardia Aristata, Bordeaux, France
34 / Croton Leaves, Seychelles
35 / Poppy, Cotswolds, England
36 / Iris, Aquitaine, France
37 / Morning Glory, Geneva, Switzerland
38 / Tulips, Russell Square, London, England
39 / Hibiscus, Pays-Basque, France
40 / Formal Garden, Catherine Palace, Tsarskoe Selo, Russia
41 / Peacock, Kew Gardens, London, England
42 / Fields in Flower, Ephesus, Turkey
43 / Tulips, Frankfurt, Germany
44 / Forest Floor, Ontario, Canada
45 / Fall Colors, New England, USA
46 / Himalayan Pink Tulip Tree
47 / Paper Lantern in Cherry Tree, Miyajima, Japan
48 / Birch Trees, Kent, England
49 / Yosemite National Park, California, USA
50 / Spring Clouds over Arabia
51 / Summer Cloud over England
52 / Blue Ceiling, Italy
53 / Lava Flow (1), Mount Etna, Sicily
54 / Lava Flow (2), Mount Etna, Sicily
55 / Aegean Sunrise, Greece
56 / Baltic Sunset, Gotland, Sweden
57 / Aegean Moon, Greece
58 / Pool, Muscat, Oman
59 / Pool (1), Hammamet, Tunisia

60 / Pool, Hearst Castle, California, USA
61 / Pool, Manama, Bahrain
62 / Blue Tiles, Italy
63 / Pool, Delhi, India
64 / Pool (2), Hammamet, Tunisia
65 / Blue Wall with Pipes, Bahrain
66 / Red and White Door, Italy
67 / Pink Metal Gate, Italy
68 / Colored Ribbons, Peace Park, Hiroshima, Japan
69 / Paving Slabs, Doha, Qatar
70 / Temple Garden, Taizo-in, Kyoto, Japan
71 / Dam on Euphrates, Al-Thawra, Syria
72 / Castle Stair, Krak des Chevaliers, Syria
73 / Greek Theater, Kourion, Cyprus
74 / Oriental Brickwork, Tozeur, Tunisia
75 / Apartment Block, Dubai, United Arab Emirates
76 / Window, Stockholm City Hall, Sweden
77 / Sandstorm, Jeddah, Saudi Arabia
78 / Station Roof, Brighton, England
79 / Social Science Research Centre, Berlin, Germany
80 / Window, London, England
81 / Blue Fence, Adriatic Coast, Italy
82 / Dome of St. Basil's, Moscow, Russia
83 / Fisherman's Hut, Gotland, Sweden
84 / Itsukushima Jinja Shrine, Miyajima, Japan